CW00859098

Modern Yoruba

A concise introduction to the Yoruba language

.

Modern Yoruba
A concise introduction to the Yoruba language

kasahorow Editors

Modern Yoruba: a concise introduction to the Yoruba language

by kasahorow Editors

Series: kasahorow Language Guides

ISBN 978-1490957661
2nd Printing
©kasahorow.org. Ka Yoruba. Lojo ojumọ.

Contents

List of Tables

Preface

All mistakes are ours.

License

You may freely photocopy and redistribute this book for private or commercial use. No restrictions. Yes you do not need our permission. Do good.

Errata

The website for this book is
        http://kasahorow.org/book/concise-yoruba.
Please submit your feedback via email at
        help@kasahorow.org.

Typesetting

This book was was typeset with XeTeX. The font is Gentium Basic.

Chapter 1

Modern Yoruba

This short guide is designed to get you up to speed quickly with the modern Yoruba language. We hope that after getting through it you will be able to read, write and speak basic Yoruba sentences to express the following range of concepts:

1. I love you
2. Kunle and Bolaji are boys
3. John came here before I did
4. Who is that?
5. Bunmi will come home tomorrow
6. I came, I saw, I conquered
7. They do not like that
8. How did they eat five pizzas in two hours?
9. The family has entered their new house

10. Stop eating and hurry up!

For teachers of Yoruba, this guide should provide you a basic outline for getting your new language learners to master the basic structure of the Yoruba language. "Modern Yoruba" is the spelling system used in this book. Regional variations are purposely omitted from this guide except in the Speaking Yoruba chapter (4).

1.1   Some explanations

In the text, any text marked with * indicates ungrammatical usage. Bolded text can be looked up in the index. The guide attempts to use plain English the first time a concept is explained; in this case the technical term is included in square brackets.

Pronunciations are surrounded by /.../ signs.

Written form   a

Spoken form   /a/

English translations are placed in italics in [ ] near their Yoruba renditions.

Chapter 2

Reading Yoruba

The easiest way to learn the rules [**grammar**] of a language is to read text written in that language. This section will help you analyse Yoruba texts to extract meaning from them.

In the past Yoruba text was written exactly the way it was spoken. This means that a lot of old material may be hard to read if you are not familiar with the pronunciation style of the writer. However, modern Yoruba is written in a consistent way regardless of the writer's pronunciation. Chapter 3 has more details of how modern Yoruba is written.

This chapter teaches you how to read modern Yoruba text.

2.1 Recognising letters

Yoruba is written with 24 letters [the Yoruba **alphabet**].

Aa	Bb	Dd	Ee	Ẹẹ
Ff	Gg	Hh	Ii	Jj
Kk	Ll	Mm	Nn	Oo
Ọọ	Pp	Rr	Ss	Ṣṣ
Tt	Uu	Ww	Yy	

Table 2.1: Yoruba alphabet

2.2 Recognising words

The main types of words [**parts of speech**] used in Yoruba are those that represent persons, places, things or ideas [**nouns**], and actions [**verbs**].

2.2.1 Nouns

The nouns in each language are unlimited. Everything that has a name is a noun. Nouns can be represented by a single word or a group of words. Languages grow by making up new nouns to refer to new things.

Whether there is just one item of the noun or the noun cannot be counted [**singular**], or whether there is more than one item of the noun [**plural**], there are no differences in spelling in Yoruba.

	Singular	Plural	Singular	Plural
Yoruba	oko	oko	molebi	molebi
English	farm	farms	family	families

2.2.2 Determiners

Definite articles come after the noun. Indefinite articles are implied.

- **definite articles**
  omokunrin **naa** [**the** boy]
  omokunrin **kan** [**some** boy]

- **indefinite articles**
  omokunrin [boy, **a** boy]
  agbalagba [adult, **an** adult];

2.2.3 Pronouns

Happily, pronouns can stand in for any noun. The common pronouns are explained below.

Subject pronouns usually replace a noun at the beginning of a sentence. A subject pronoun is the initiator of a verb's action. It usually comes before a verb.

Yoruba	emi, mo ∼	iwọ ∼	ohun ∼
English	I	you	she, he, it
Yoruba	awa ∼	ẹyin ∼	awọn ∼
English	we	you (plural)	they

Table 2.2: Subject pronouns

The verb replaces the tilde '∼' after the pronoun 2.2, for example, **Emi** *ni ifẹ rẹ* [*I love you*]. In older texts, the pronoun is usually written together with the verb as **Monifẹrẹ**.

Yoruba	mi	e	ohun
English	me	you	her, him, it
Yoruba	wa	yin	wọn
English	us	you (plural)	them

Table 2.3: Object pronouns.

Object pronouns usually replace a noun anywhere else apart from in the beginning of a sentence. Object pronouns, listed in Table 2.3, are written alone, for example, Gba fun **mi** [*Get it for **me***].

Possesive pronouns attribute ownership to someone or something. Possessive pronouns, listed in table 2.4, are written alone, for example, ohunje **mi** [**my** food].

Interrogative pronouns, listed in Table 2.5, are used to ask questions, for example, **Tani** oun? [***Who** is he/she?*].

Yoruba	mi	rẹ	ohun
English	my	your	her, his, its
Yoruba	wa	yin	wọn
English	our	your (plural)	their

Table 2.4: Possessive pronouns.

Yoruba	English
tani	who
kini	what
kilo fa	why
nibo	where
bawo	how
ewo	which

Table 2.5: Interrogative pronouns.

2.2.4 Verbs

There are two important things to look for in Yoruba verbs:

- an indication of the period of time in which the action took place [**tense**],

- an indication of whether the opposite action is being described [**negation**].

Action taking place now or habitually

For actions taking place at the time of speaking [**simple present tense**], or that take place on a regular basis [**habitual tense**], the verb has no special indicator

11

of time. This is the form of the verb found in dictionary entries.

Yoruba	Mo **wa**	Kunle **wa**
English	I **come**	Kunle **comes**
Yoruba	Mo **o** wa	Kunle **o** wa
English	I **don't** come	Kunle **doesn't** come

Table 2.6: Simple present, habitual tense.

Action took place in the past

This is the **simple past tense**.

Yoruba	Mo **wa** lana	Tunde **wa** lana
English	I **came** yesterday	Tunde **came** yesterday
Yoruba	Mo **o** wa	Tunde **o** wa
English	I **didn't** come	Tunde **didn't** come

Table 2.7: Simple past tense.

Action has taken place

This is the **present perfect tense**. The present perfect tense is indicated by inserting **ti** [*has, have*] in front of the verb.

Action is taking place

This is the **present continuous tense**. It is indicated by inserting **n** [*is in the process of*] in front of the verb.

12

Yoruba	Mo **ti** wa	Funmi **ti** wa
English	I **have** come	Funmi **has** come
Yoruba	Mo **o** ti wa	Funmi **o** ti wa
English	I have **not** come	Funmi has **not** come

Table 2.8: Present perfect tense.

Yoruba	Mo **n**wa	Kemi **n**wa
English	I **am** coming	Kemi **is** coming
Yoruba	Mo **o** nwa	Kemi **o** nwa
English	I am **not** coming	Kemi is **not** coming

Table 2.9: Present continuous tense.

Action will take place in the future

This is the **simple future tense.**The future tense is indicated by inserting **ma** [*will*] in front of the verb.

Yoruba	Mo **ma** wa	Kemi **ma** wa
English	I **will** come	Kemi **will** come
Yoruba	Mo **o** ma wa	Kemi **o** ma wa
English	I will **not** come	Kemi will **not** come

Table 2.10: Future tense.

A good verb conjugation book will give you plenty of practice in forming negations of the various verb tenses.

2.2.5   Extending Nouns and Verbs

Nouns and verbs can be extended in meaning with additional words.

Nouns are extended with **adjectives**. Adjectives are placed after the noun. For example, ile **tuntun** [**new house**].

Verbs can be extended in meaning with **adverbs**. Adverbs are also placed after the verb. For example, rin **kiakia** [walk **quickly**].

Adjectives and adverbs have the unique property that they can be repeated for emphasis.

	Adjective	Adverb
Yoruba	dun ,	kia
English	sweet	quick(ly)
Yoruba	dun pupọ	kiakia
English	very sweet	very quick(ly)
Yoruba	dun pupọ pupọ	kiakiakia
English	very very sweet	very very quick(ly)

Table 2.11: Repeat for emphasis.

2.3   Recognising sentences

There are three main sentence patterns in Yoruba:

- making a statement [**declarative sentences**]

- asking a question [**interrogative sentences**]

- commanding [**imperative sentences**]

Making a statement

e.g. *I love you.*

Yoruba Word Order	Mo	ni ife	re
Grammar	[Noun]	[Verb]	[Noun]
	required	*required*	*optional*
Literal English	I	have loved	you

Asking a question

e.g. *How are you?*

Yoruba Word Order	Bawo	ni?
Grammar	[Pronoun]	[Verb]
	required	*optional*
Literal English*	How	is it?

Commanding

e.g. *Stop making noise!*

Yoruba Word Order	Duro	ariwo!
Grammar	[Verb]	[Verb]
	required	*required*
Literal English*	Stop	noise-making!

2.3.1 Forming complex sentences

Conjunctions allow you to link nouns or verbs. Some common conjunctions are listed in Table 2.12.

Yoruba	Kunle **ati** Kemi	Jẹun **ko** sun
English	Kunle **with** Kemi	Eat **then** sleep
English	Kunle **and** Kemi	Eat **and** sleep
Yoruba	Kunle **tabi** Kemi	Mo nsun **nibayi** sun
English	Kunle **or** Kemi	I am sleeping **so** sleep
Yoruba	**Ti** Ade ...	**Ti** Ade ba **wa**, ...
English	**If** Ade ...	**If** Ade comes **then** ...
Yoruba	**Nwon ba** mo ...	**Biba ti** ẹ sun ...
English	**While** I ...	**Even if** I sleep ...

Table 2.12: Common conjunctions.

The following sentence patterns therefore should be easy to understand:

Kunle nlọ <u>ile-iwe</u>.
[*Kunle is going to <u>school</u>.*]

<u>Kunle ati Kemi</u> nlọ ile-iwe.
<u>Kunle and Kemi</u> are going to school.

Kunle ati Kemi nsun <u>ki won</u> to lọ ile-iwe.
Kunle and Kemi are sleeping <u>before</u> they go to school.

Chapter 3

Writing Modern Yoruba

The philosophy behind this updated orthography is that written Yoruba should be more predictable than spoken Yoruba, yet be sufficiently pliable to allow the writer to capture shades of meaning without undue exertion.

So Modern Yoruba strives to achieve a noticeable aesthetic of simplicity of form and elegance of construction as exemplified by the great proverbs of the Yoruba people.

3.1 Spelling conventions

The following spelling conventions are supported by the spellchecker available from the Yoruba language resources page at http://kasahorow.org/yoruba.

3.2 General guidelines

- Do not use accents on top of vowels [**diacritics**]. Instead structure your sentences to avoid ambiguity. For example, write **Sọ Yoruba lojo ojumọ** [*Box A is bigger than box B*] instead of **Sọ Yòrùbá lójo ojúmọ́***. The version without diacritics is easier to write and just as clear and unambiguous.

- Do not use elliptical forms. Write **ohun njeun** [*he is eating*] instead of **ohunjeun*** or **ounjeun***. This serves the purpose of making text easier to break down after a single read (Table **??**).

- Hyphenate words joined together to form a single concept to clarify the composition of the new concept. For example, **ile-iwe** [*house of book***] is preferred to **ileiwe***

3.3   Importing foreign words

- Import into Yoruba, without a change of spelling, specialised terminology unlikely to come into popular usage. This eliminates the possibility of ambiguity for specialists who are already familiar with the term.

- Phonetically render into Yoruba new words likely to come into popular usage. When doing so, stick to the pronunciation pattern of the original language. This enables readers who encounter the word for the first-time in writing to pronounce the word in a way that will confirm to their ears that it is indeed not an uncommon term. For example, **intanẹt** [*internet*].

  When words are deemed to have made the transition from specialised terminology into popular usage, this convention should be applied to revise the spelling of the word accordingly.

Chapter 4

Speaking Yoruba

4.1   Sounds

The sounds in Yoruba are divided into **vowels** and **consonants**. There are seven vowels in Yoruba—a e ẹ i o ọ u—representing ten sounds as listed in Table 4.1.

Nasalized vowels are not included here as you typically don't need them to make yourself understood.

Written	Sound	As in
a	/a/	h**a**t
e	/ay/	s**ay**
ẹ	/ɛ/	h**e**n
i	/i/	f**ee**d
o	/o/	g**oa**t
ọ	/ɔ/	h**o**t
u	/u/	c**oo**l

Table 4.1: Yoruba vowels and their pronunciation.

The following sentence contains all the Yoruba vowel sounds:

Mo	fẹ	lọ	jẹ	fufu
M/o/	f/ɛ/	l/ɔ/	j/ɛ/	f/u/fu
ati	ewedu	pẹlu	ẹran	igbẹ
/a/t/i/	/e/wedu	pẹlu	ẹran	igbẹ

The rest of the Yoruba alphabet represent the consonants. They are enunciated in the same way as the English pronunciation of those letters. Additional consonants are represented by the combinations

digraphs

listed in 4.2. The sound combination is enunciated as a single short sound.

Written	Sound	As in
gb	/gb/	Digby
ṣ	/sh/	shine

Table 4.2: Yoruba digraphs and their pronunciation.

Yoruba writing	Sound	As in
b	/b/	ban
d	/d/	din
f	/f/	fan
g	/g/	go
h	/h/	hi
j	/j/	jut
k	/k/	kin
l	/l/	lit
m	/m/	mum
n	/n/	nun
p	/p/	pun
r	/r/	run
s	/s/	son
t	/t/	ton
w	/w/	wan
y	/y/	yes
z	/z/	zoo

Table 4.3: Yoruba consonants and their pronunciation.

4.2 Listening to Yoruba

You should now be able to understand basic Yoruba with the aid of a dictionary.

Typically, if you cannot follow spoken speech, ask the speaker to slow down their rate of talking. At the slower speed, you should be able to pick up enough words to make sense of what is being said. (You only need to ask them to speak louder if they are speaking too softly.)

Chapter 5

Phrase Reference

Here are some handy phrases that you should memorize to fill in the silence while you frantically think of how to say something complicated.

Hello	Bawo?
How are you?	Bawo ni?
I am fine	Mo wa dada
And you?	Iwọ nko?
Goodbye	Odabọ
Later	Nigbami
Good morning	Ka arọ
Good afternoon	Ka san
Good evening	Ku rọlẹ
Good night	Odarọ
Sleep well	Sun dada

What is your name?	Kini orukọ rẹ?
My name is Janet	Orukọ mi Janet
I come from France	Ati Faranse ni mo ti wa
I am a ...	... ni mi
I am a teacher	Olukọ ni mi
I am hungry	Ebi npa mi
I am thirsty	Ohungbẹ ngbẹ mi
I like/want ...	Mo fẹ ...
I don't like/want ...	Mi o fẹ ...
It is a bit expensive	O han diẹ
It is not expensive	Ko han
Yes	Bẹẹni
No	Bẹẹko; Rara
Please	Jọọ; Dakun
Sorry	Pẹlẹ
Thank you	Ọṣe
What is the time?	Ago melo lo ti lu?
The time is ...	Ago ...
The time is 2 o'clock	Ago meji ti lu

Congratulations! Go and explore the world in Yoruba!

Chapter 6

Basic Vocabulary

A

aalọ (n) riddle
i.e. puzzles and riddles

aanu (n) empathy
i.e. she has such empathy

Abamẹta (n) Saturday
i.e. Saturday children

abẹ (n) razor
i.e. sharpen the razor

abẹẹrẹ (n) syringe
i.e. a nurse's syringe

abẹrẹ (n) injection
i.e. an injection is painful

abẹrẹ (n) needle
i.e. string and needle

abiya (n) armpit
i.e. smelly armpit

abọ (n) consequence
i.e. its consequences

abọ (n) plate
i.e. wash your plate

aburo mi obinrin (n) sister
i.e. my only sister

ada (n) cutlass
i.e. give me the cutlass

adajọ (n) judge
i.e. seven judges

adayeba (n) history
i.e. learn history

adiyẹ (n) chicken
i.e. chicken meat

afikun (n) addition
i.e. 1 + 1 = 2; this is addition

afipe (n) title
i.e. "Mighty One" is a title

aga (n) chair
i.e. arrange the chairs

agba (adj) elder
i.e. my elder sibling

agba (n) barrel
i.e. fill up the barrel

agbado (n) corn
i.e. corn and groundnuts

agbagba (n) plantain
i.e. plantain and cassava

agbalagba (n) adult
i.e. he is an adult

agbami (n) sea
i.e. a river goes into a sea

agbara (n) power
i.e. strength and power
agbarigo (n) lorry
i.e. lorry stop
agbẹ (n) farmer
i.e. she is a farmer
agbọn (n) chin
i.e. hold your chin
agbon (n) chin
i.e. hold your chin
Agẹmọ (n) July
i.e. July has 31 days
ago (n) coop
i.e. hen coop
agunfọn (n) giraffe
i.e. a giraffe is an animal

aguntan (n) sheep
i.e. sheep meat (i.e. mutton)
aida (n) evil
i.e. which evil is this?
aidirogini (n) hydrogen
i.e. hydrogen car
Aiku (n) Sunday
i.e. Kwasi and Akosua are Sunday children
aimojukuro (n) covetuousness

i.e. covetuousness is not good
aja (n) dog
i.e. a dog barks
ajagun (n) soldier
i.e. the soldiers are marching
Aje (n) Monday
i.e. Monday children
ajẹ (n) witchcraft
i.e. practise witchcraft
ajeji (n) foreigner
i.e. the foreigners have arrived
ajẹku (n) waste
i.e. the work has been a waste
ajinde (n) resurrection
i.e. the resurrection of Christ
akaba (n) ladder
i.e. long ladder
akọ (n) paddle
i.e. canoe and paddle
akọgba (n) fence
i.e. behind a fence
akukọ (n) cockerel
i.e. a cockerel is crowing

alaafia (n) peace
   i.e. I want peace
alafia (n) comfort
   i.e. give me comfort
alailopin (n) infinity
   i.e. if you divide any number by zero, you get infinity
alaisan (n) patient
   i.e. the patients sleep here

alangba (n) lizard
   i.e. a lizard eats grass
alara ẹran (n) humankind
   i.e. we are humankind
alẹ (n) night
   i.e. 8 o'clock in the night

ale (n) concubine
   i.e. Yaa is my concubine

alegba (n) alligator
   i.e. an alligator has a tail

alejo (n) guest
   i.e. I am a guest
Algeria (n) Algeria
   i.e. go to Algeria

ami (n) sign
   i.e. a sign of hope
amọ (n) mud
   i.e. wash the mud
amọn (n) clay
   i.e. clay vase
ana (n) in-law
   i.e. our in-laws
apa (n) arm
   i.e. lift up your arm
apa (n) philanderer
   i.e. you have made yourself a philanderer
apaniyan (n) murderer
   i.e. he is a murderer
apẹja (n) fisherman
   i.e. he is a fisherman
apẹrẹ (n) basket
   i.e. carry a basket
apo (n) bag
   i.e. look at the bag
apoti (n) box
   i.e. box A is bigger than box B
apoti (n) stool
   i.e. sit on the stool
ara ẹran (n) flesh
   i.e. flesh and blood

arakunrin (n) brother
i.e. my only brother
ariwo (n) noise
i.e. stop making noise
arọ (n) morning
i.e. early morning
arugbo (adj) old
i.e. old pan
arun (n) disease
i.e. heal disease
asẹ (n) collander
i.e. use the collander to drain the rice
asẹ (n) will
i.e. God's will
asẹmale (n) muslim
i.e. a Christian and a Muslim
asiko (n) duration
i.e. forty-hour duration

asiko (n) moment
i.e. the moment is up
asiko (n) time
i.e. the time is up
asọ (n) dress
i.e. blue dress
asọ (n) attire
i.e. your attire is beauti-

ful
asọ (n) garment
i.e. wear a garment
asọ ibora (n) blanket
i.e. wet blanket
asọ inura (n) towel
i.e. wet towel
asọrọmagbesi (n) radio
i.e. switch on the radio
asun (n) khebab
i.e. khebabs and beer
atẹgun lile (n) storm
i.e. storm with thunder
ati (conj) and
i.e. Kofi and Ama
awo eeru (adj) brown
i.e. brown bird
awọn (det) the
i.e. the house
awọn era (n) ants
i.e. the ants are thriving

aworan (n) picture
i.e. beautiful picture
aya (n) missus
i.e. Missus Clinton
aya (n) chest
i.e. chest hair

ayanfẹ (n) beloved
i.e. my beloved has tricked me

ayelujara (n) link
i.e. Internet link

ayẹyẹ (n) event
i.e. the event has started

B

baaṣi (n) waache
i.e. waache and cowhide

baba (n) father
i.e. my father's child is my sibling

baba (n) father
i.e. my father's child is my sibling

baba arugbo (n) old man
i.e. he is an old man

bata (n) shoe
i.e. wear your shoes

Belu (n) November
i.e. November has 30 days

bere (v) ask
i.e. ask Kofi

bi (adv) as
i.e. as it is

bọlẹkaja (n) van
i.e. board a van

bọọlu (n) ball
i.e. play ball

burẹdi (n) bread
i.e. soft bread

C

ceedi (n) cedi
i.e. hundred pesewas make one cedi

D

da duro (n) inactive
i.e. he is inactive

daya (n) toffee
i.e. lick a toffee

de (v) arrive
i.e. when you arrive, call me

diẹ (adj) little
i.e. pour a little liquor

dimọ (v) embrace
i.e. embrace me

dingi (n) mirror
  i.e. big mirror
dudu (adj) black
  i.e. black cloth
ẹ (p) you
  i.e. you eat
ẹbi (n) family
  i.e. new family

E

ebi (n) hunger
  i.e. hunger and thirst
ẹbi (n) relative
  i.e. he is a relative
Ẹbibi (n) May
  i.e. May has 31 days
ẹbọ (n) sacrifice
  i.e. offer a sacrifice
ẹbun (n) gift
  i.e. a good gift
ẹbun (n) award
  i.e. give her an award
ẹda (n) creation
  i.e. all creation
ede ayede (n) quarrel
  i.e. a big quarrel
ẹẹdan (n) falsification
  i.e. lies and falsifications

eedu (n) charcoal
  i.e. sack of charcoal
ẹgbẹ (n) group
  i.e. let us found a group
ẹgbẹ (n) association
  i.e. come to the men's association meeting
egbo (n) sore
  i.e. the dog is licking its sore
ege (n) cassava
  i.e. plantain and cassava

ẹiyẹ (n) bird
  i.e. a bird flies
ẹja (n) fish
  i.e. fried fish
ẹjẹ (n) oath
  i.e. great oath
ẹjẹ (n) blood
  i.e. water and blood
ejo (n) snake
  i.e. a snake has no legs
ẹkọ (n) education
  i.e. health and education

ekurọ (n) palmnut wool
  i.e. palmnut wool burns

well
ẹlẹda (n) creator
  i.e. creator god
elubọ (n) flour
  i.e. corn flour
emi (n) self
  i.e. myself, yourself
ẹmi (n) soul
  i.e. my soul exults
ẹmi (n) spirit
  i.e. he has a strong spirit

eniyan (n) human
  i.e. we are humans
ẹnu (n) mouth
  i.e. my mouth
ẹnu (n) lips
  i.e. red lips
ẹpa (n) groundnut
  i.e. corn and groundnuts

era (n) ant
  i.e. thousands of ants
ẹran (n) beef
  i.e. eat beef
ẹran (n) meat
  i.e. goat meat
ere (n) doll
  i.e. my doll

ere idaraya (n) game
  i.e. play a game
ere idije (n) competition
  i.e. football competition

Erele (n) February
  i.e. February has 28 or
  29 days
Ẹrẹna (n) March
  i.e. March has 31 days
erin (n) elephant
  i.e. an elephant is very
  big
ẹrọ (n) machine
  i.e. new machine
ẹrọ (n) tap
  i.e. open the tap
ero (n) crowd
  i.e. noisy crowd
ẹrọ ayilujara (n) internet
  i.e. internet link
ero ọkan (n) disposition
  i.e. a person's disposition

ẹru (n) fear
  i.e. fear has filled her heart

eru (n) ash
  i.e. charcoal and ashes

erupẹ (n) sand
i.e. beach sand

ẹsẹ (n) leg
i.e. swollen foot

ẹṣin (n) horse
i.e. white horse

eso (n) fruit
i.e. pluck fruit

esuke (n) hiccups
i.e. he has got the hiccups

ẹsun (n) accusation
i.e. lay an accusation

ẹtan (n) deception
i.e. deception and discord

Ẹti (n) Friday
i.e. Friday children

eti okun (n) beach
i.e. beach sand

eti tente (n) ledge
i.e. sleep on the ledge

eto (n) table
i.e. chair and table

ẹtu (n) deer
i.e. a lion likes deer meat

ẹwa (n) bean
i.e. rice and beans

ẹwa (n) beauty
i.e. beauty and love

ewe (n) leaf
i.e. green leaf

ewe koko (n) cocoyam leaves
i.e. cocoyam leaves stew

eweko (n) plant
i.e. red plant

ẹwọn (n) jail
i.e. go to jail

ẹwọn (n) prison
i.e. go to prison

ewu (n) cloth
i.e. sew cloth

ẹya (n) version
i.e. which version?

ẹyawo (n) loan
i.e. I need a loan

ẹyẹ (n) bird
i.e. a bird flies

ẹyin (n) egg
i.e. chicken egg

ẹyin-kule (n) backyard
i.e. the backyard is overgrown

F

fadaka (n) coin
  i.e. four coins
fẹ (v) blow
  i.e. blow air
ferese (n) window
  i.e. open the windows
fideo (n) video
  i.e. watch the video
fila (n) hat
  i.e. he is wearing a hat
fimọ (v) attach
  i.e. attach to wall
finusọkan (v) agree
  i.e. do you agree?
fo (n) fly
  i.e. a fly flies
fo (v) clean
  i.e. clean your teeth
funfun (adj) white
  i.e. white house

G

gan gan (n) gong gong
  i.e. play the gong gong
gangan (n) talking drum
  i.e. four talking drums
gba (v) accept
  i.e. accept her

gbangba (n) public
  i.e. you don't say 'vagina'
  in public
gbeborun (n) gossip
  i.e. gossip is not good
gbogbo (det) all
  i.e. all things
gele (n) headgear
  i.e. put on headgear
gọta (n) gutter
  i.e. there is water in the
  gutter

H

halahala (n) groin
  i.e. groin of a man

I

ibi (n) here
  i.e. go from here
iboji (n) shade
  i.e. I am sitting under the
  shade
ibugbe (n) habitat
  i.e. habitat of animals
ibugbe (n) lodge
  i.e. stay at the lodging
  for a while

ibukun (n) blessing
  i.e. God's blessing
ibusun (n) bed
  i.e. sleep on the bed
idaduro (n) sabotage
  i.e. this is sabotage
idajọ (n) judgement
  i.e. which judgement?
idamu () worry
  i.e. many worries
idanwo (n) exam
  i.e. the exam is easy
idanwo (n) test
  i.e. the test is difficult
idariji (n) forgiveness
  i.e. love, acceptance and forgiveness
idi (n) bum
  i.e. large bum
idi (n) reason
  i.e. everything has a reason
idorogun (n) rivalry
  i.e. stop the rivalry
idọti (n) rubbish
  i.e. throw away the rubbish
idọti (n) trash
  i.e. throw away the trash

idunnu (n) happiness
  i.e. happiness has arrived

ife (n) cup
  i.e. tea cup
ifiyin fun (n) exultation
  i.e. songs of exultation
ifọkansi (n) determination
  i.e. we will do it with determination
iforiti (n) hope
  i.e. I have hope
igba (n) garden egg
  i.e. garden egg stew
igbagbe (n) forgetfulness
  i.e. her forgetfulness
igbagbọ (n) faith
  i.e. faith and peace
igbagbo (n) christian
  i.e. a Christian and a Muslim
igbalẹ (n) broom
  i.e. broom and dustpan
Igbe (n) April
  i.e. April has 30 days
igbega (n) glory
  i.e. glory of humankind

igbin (n) snail
i.e. I eat snails

igbo (n) bush
i.e. go into the bush

igboro (n) town
i.e. go into town

igi (n) stick
i.e. break the stick

igi (n) tree
i.e. plant a tree

igi ifoyin (n) toothbrush
i.e. toothbrush and toothpaste

igo (n) bottle
i.e. five bottles

igun (n) vulture
i.e. a vulture is a bird

iho (n) hole
i.e. small hole

ijapa (n) tortoise
i.e. a tortoise walks slowly

ijiyan (n) argument
i.e. many arguments

ijoba (n) government
i.e. Nkrumah's govern-
ment

ika (n) wickedness
i.e. your stinginess and
your wickedness

ika (n) finger
i.e. show me your finger

ikarahun (n) shell
i.e. shell of a crab

ike (n) bucket
i.e. the bucket leaks

ikebe (n) buttocks
i.e. big buttocks

ikede (n) announcement
i.e. read the announce-
ment

ikole (n) dustpan
i.e. broom and dustpan

ikolu ara eni (n) friction
i.e. friction came between
us

ikun (n) abdomen
i.e. abdomen of a dog

ilara (n) hatred
i.e. hatred has no cure

ile (n) floor
i.e. on the floor

ile (n) house
i.e. the house

ile (n) home
i.e. your home

ilẹ (n) land
 i.e. buy land
ile ijosin (n) church
 i.e. go to church
ile itura (n) hotel
 i.e. she sleeps at a hotel
ile iwẹ (n) bathroom
 i.e. go to the bathroom
ile-iwe (n) school
 i.e. I learn to read at school

ilẹkun (n) door
 i.e. close the door
ilẹkun (n) door
 i.e. close the door
ilera (n) health
 i.e. food gives health
ileri (n) promise
 i.e. promise me
ilu (n) nation
 i.e. your nation
ilu (n) drum
 i.e. I hear the drums
imọran (n) advice
 i.e. a priest has advice
imu (n) nose
 i.e. ear and nose
inunibini (n) enmity
 i.e. great enmity

inunibini (n) discord
 i.e. lies and discord
ipaniyan (n) murder
 i.e. gossip and murder
ipe (n) message
 i.e. when the message arrived
ipejọpọ (n) meeting
 i.e. cancel the meeting
ipilẹ (n) foundation
 i.e. foundation of the house

ipo (n) state
 i.e. look at our pitiful state

iranwọ (n) help
 i.e. everyone needs help

irawọ (n) star
 i.e. plenty of stars
irẹ (n) porcupine
 i.e. porcupine hole
irin (n) metal
 i.e. hat of metal
irọ (n) lie
 i.e. lies and discord
irọlẹ (n) evening
 i.e. evening meal; dinner

irora (n) pain
i.e. the pain is here
iroyin (n) news
i.e. news of the realm
irun (n) hair
i.e. chest hair
irun oju (n) eyebrow
i.e. eye and eyebrow
iṣe (n) poverty
i.e. poverty or wealth
iṣe (n) act
i.e. Act One
iṣẹ (n) work
i.e. I want work I would do
iṣẹ (n) blow
i.e. give him a blow
iṣẹ ṣiṣe (n) working
i.e. working is not trivial
Isẹgun (n) Tuesday
i.e. Tuesday children
iṣeju (n) minute
i.e. five minutes
iṣere (n) swing
i.e. play on a swing
iṣeyun (n) abortion
i.e. the doctor performs abortion

isin (n) service
i.e. thanksgiving service
isinku (n) funeral
i.e. I am going to a funeral
iṣiro (n) accounts
i.e. she made accounts
iṣo (n) nail
i.e. plank and nail
isọdọmọ (n) adoption
i.e. give her up for adoption
iṣu (n) yam
i.e. cook the yam
ita (n) outdoors
i.e. go outdoors
itanran (n) compensation
i.e. have you received your compensation?
itẹwọgba (n) acceptance
i.e. love, acceptance and forgiveness
itiju (n) disgrace
i.e. shame and disgrace
itiju (n) shame
i.e. shame and disgrace
iwa (n) habit
i.e. bad habit

iwa (n) character
i.e. her character
iwaju ori (n) forehead
i.e. look at her forehead

iwe (n) book
i.e. this book
iwe (n) book
i.e. this book
iwe (n) paper
i.e. today's paper
iwe-eri (n) certificate
i.e. when you complete school you get a certificate
iwọ (p) you
i.e. you eat
iwoju (n) mirror
i.e. big mirror
iwọn giramu (n) gramme
i.e. ten grammes
iya (n) mother
i.e. my mother's child is my sibling
iya arugbo (n) old lady
i.e. my old lady
iyanju (n) encouragement
i.e. encouragement and joy

iyara (n) activity
i.e. there are many activities there
iyara ibusun (n) bedroom
i.e. the house has two bedrooms
iyara idana (n) kitchen
i.e. I am in the kitchen
iyarun (n) comb
i.e. use a comb to comb your hair
iyarun (n) comb
i.e. use a comb to comb your hair
iyawo (n) wife
i.e. my wife and my children
iyawo (n) bride
i.e. bride's husband; groom

iyẹ (n) feather
i.e. bird's feathers
iyẹpẹ (n) stone
i.e. stones and cement

J

jagun (v) battle
i.e. we are going to bat-

tle them
jagunjagun (n) warrior
  i.e. warrior of antiquity

jama (n) jama
  i.e. sing jama
je (v) chew
  i.e. to chew groundnuts

jẹ (v) eat
  i.e. to eat everything
jiyan (v) argue
  i.e. argue with him
jo (v) burn
  i.e. burn papers
joko (v) sit
  i.e. to sit here
jọlọfu (n) jollof
  i.e. jollof is food

K

ka (v) read
  i.e. to read a book
kẹkẹ (n) bicycle
  i.e. new bicycle
kibọọdu (n) keyboard
  i.e. press "k" on the keyboard

kilomita (n) kilometer
  i.e. ten kilometers
kilomita (n) kilometre
  i.e. ten kilometres
ko (v) build
  i.e. build a house
koko (n) cocoa
  i.e. cocoa tree
kọkọrọ (n) key
  i.e. door and key
kọmpiyuta (n) computer
  i.e. computer keyboard
kọnga (n) well
  i.e. well water
kooṣi (n) coach
  i.e. a football team coach

kootu (n) court
  i.e. I am going to court
koriko (n) grass
  i.e. a cow chews grass
koto (n) pit
  i.e. dig a pit

L

labalaba (n) butterfly
  i.e. a butterfly is beautiful

lati (prep) from
  i.e. go from here
lawọ (n) generosity
  i.e. your generosity
lẹhin (prep) behind
  i.e. go behind
lẹhin odi (n) abroad
  i.e. she goes abroad
lẹkansi (adv) again
  i.e. see her again
lẹnsi (n) lens
  i.e. lens of a camera
lọ (v) go
  i.e. to go to school
lu (v) beat
  i.e. beat someone

M

maalu (n) cow
  i.e. cow meat; beef
maapu (n) map
  i.e. read the map
maili (n) mile
  i.e. ten miles
mi (p) my
  i.e. my house
mimọyi (n) appreciative-
  ness

  i.e. show your apprecia-
  tiveness
mita (n) metre
  i.e. five kilometers
mita (n) meter
  i.e. ten meters
mo (p) I
  i.e. I eat
mọ (n) light
  i.e. light of the sky
mọyi (v) appreciate
  i.e. you do not appreciate this
muṣere (n) diss
  i.e. it is not a diss

N

naa (det) the
  i.e. the house
ni (prep) at
  i.e. meet me at home
nkan (n) thing
  i.e. the thing; the things

nọsẹ (n) stroll
  i.e. take a stroll
nọwonọwo (n) philanthropist
  i.e. she is a philanthropist

nṣẹjẹ (n) bleeding
  i.e. stop the bleeding

O

o (p) it
  i.e. it falls
o (p) you
  i.e. you eat
ọba (n) king
  i.e. he is a king
ọbẹ (n) knife
  i.e. sharpen a knife
ọbẹ (n) stew
  i.e. make stew
ọbẹ (n) soup
  i.e. palm nut soup
obi (n) parents
  i.e. his parents
ọbinrin (n) woman
  i.e. a pretty woman
ọda (n) ink
  i.e. ink in a pen
ọdẹ (n) fool
  i.e. Fool! Dimwit!
odo (n) mortar
  i.e. pestle and mortar

odo (n) river
  i.e. a river goes into a sea
odo (n) pestle
  i.e. pestle and mortar
odo (n) lake
  i.e. the lake has overflowed

ododo (n) flower
  i.e. pretty flower
ọdun (n) year
  i.e. a new year has come

ọfa (n) arrow
  i.e. bow and arrow
ọfun (n) throat
  i.e. clear your throat
ọgba (n) yard
  i.e. big yard
ọgẹdẹ (n) plantain
  i.e. plantain and cassava

ọgẹdẹ wẹrẹ (n) banana
  i.e. a monkey likes bananas
ogiri (n) wall
  i.e. sit on the wall
ogun (n) inheritance
  i.e. claim your inheritance

ogun (n) battle
i.e. we are going to war

Ogun (n) August
i.e. August has 31 days

ohun (p) she
i.e. she eats

ohun (n) voice
i.e. soften your voice

ohun ojiji (n) surprise
i.e. great surprise

ohunka (n) reading
i.e. repeat the reading

ohunworan (n) spectator
i.e. the spectators

oja (n) market
i.e. go to market

ojępe (n) messenger
i.e. the messengers arrived

ojọ ibi (n) birthday
i.e. today is my birthday

Ojọbọ (n) Thursday
i.e. Thursday children

Ojọru (n) Wednesday
i.e. Wednesday children

oju (n) face
i.e. look at my face

oju (n) eye
i.e. eye and eyebrow

oju ọgbẹ (n) scar
i.e. her cheek has a scar

oju ọjọ (n) daybreak
i.e. daybreak and night-fall

ojumọ (n) day
i.e. the day has arrived

ọkan (n) heart
i.e. good heart

ọkan (n) mind
i.e. her mind

oke (n) hill
i.e. hill top

ọkọ (n) boat
i.e. red boat

ọkọ (n) husband
i.e. I love my husband

oko (n) farm
i.e. cocoa farm

ọkọ (n) hoe
i.e. hoe and cutlass

ọkọ ayọkẹlẹ (n) car
i.e. drive a car

ọkọ ofurufu (n) plane
i.e. board a plane

ọkọ ofurufu (n) aeroplane
i.e. two aeroplanes

oko oju omi (n) canoe
i.e. canoe and paddle

oku (n) corpse
i.e. the corpse is rotting

oku (n) ghost
i.e. I see a ghost

Okudu (n) June
i.e. June has 30 days

okun (n) strength
i.e. strength and power

ọkunrin (n) man
i.e. a tall man

ole (n) burglary
i.e. burglary is increasing

ologbo (n) cat
i.e. a cat has a tail

olori (n) leader
i.e. this is our leader

olori (n) queen
i.e. she is a queen

olori awọn alufa (n) bishop
i.e. she is a bishop

olu (n) mushroom
i.e. mushroom soup

omidan (n) lady
i.e. Lady Danso

omije (n) tear
i.e. my eyes filled with tears

ọmikin (n) grease
i.e. grease in a pan

ominira (n) independence
i.e. independence day

ọmọ (n) child
i.e. my mother's child is my sibling

ọmọ-ọwọ (n) baby
i.e. I have a baby

ọmọbinrin (n) girl
i.e. tall girl

ọmọde (n) toddler
i.e. toddler, where are you going?

ọmọdọ (n) maid
i.e. she is a maid

ọmọkunrin (n) boy
i.e. the boy is here

omonilu (n) citizen
i.e. I am a citizen

ọnigbagbo (n) Christianity

i.e. Christianity and Is-
lam

onilo (n) user
i.e. how many users?

onje (n) food
i.e. eat food

oogun (n) medicine
i.e. bitter medicine

ọọni (n) crocodile
i.e. a crocodile likes water

oorun (n) smell
i.e. I sense a smell

Ọpẹ (n) December
i.e. December has 31 days

opin (n) end
i.e. the end has come

ọpọlọ (n) frog
i.e. a frog likes water

opurọ (n) liar
i.e. three liars

ọrẹ (n) friend
i.e. my friend

ọrẹ (n) present
i.e.

ori (n) head
i.e. your big head

ori ewe (n) page
i.e. open page twenty-
two

origun (n) corners
i.e. all corners of the world

oriire (n) congratulations
i.e. congratulations and
well done

orilẹ aye (n) earth
i.e. people of the earth

orilẹ ede (n) continent
i.e. African continent

orisa (n) god
i.e. dependable god

ororo (n) vegetable oil
i.e. use vegetable oil to
fry fish

orun (n) sun
i.e. the sun is shining

orunkun (n) knee
i.e. my knees

ọsan (n) orange
i.e. three oranges

ọsan (n) afternoon
i.e. high afternoon

ọsẹ (n) soap
i.e. pail and soap

ọsẹ (n) soap
i.e. pail and soap
ọsẹ ifoyin (n) toothpaste
i.e. toothbrush and toothpaste
oṣo (n) wizard
i.e. he is a wizard
oṣukpa (n) moon
i.e. moon and stars
oṣuwọn (n) quantity
i.e. quantity of the food
ọta (n) enemy
i.e. enemies will tire
ọti (n) liquor
i.e. pour a little liquor
Ọwara (n) October
i.e. October has 31 days
Owewe (n) September
i.e. September has 30 days

owiwi (n) owl
i.e. an owl is a bird
ọwọ (n) hand
i.e. lift up your hand
owo (n) fees
i.e. school fees
ọwọ (n) respect
i.e. show respect

owo (n) money
i.e. money helps
owo ori (n) levy
i.e. pay a levy
oye (n) chieftain
i.e. she is a chieftain
ọyọkẹrẹ (n) sluggard
i.e. the sluggard is asleep

ọyọn (n) breast
i.e. breast milk

P

pa (v) kill
i.e. to kill a goat
paki (n) cassava
i.e. plantain and cassava
palẹmọ (n) preparation
i.e. make preparation
pasiwọọdu (n) password
i.e. change password
peeli (n) pail
i.e. pail and soap
pẹtẹẹsi (n) storey build-
ing
i.e. I am building a storey
building

pinpin (n) division
  i.e. 2/1 = 2; this is division
pondoro (n) jar
  i.e. seven jars
pọnmọ (n) cowhide
  i.e. waache and cowhide

pọsu (n) puzzle
  i.e. puzzles and riddles
pupa (adj) red
  i.e. red lips

R

reluwe (n) train
  i.e. new train
rẹwa (adj) beautiful
  i.e. it is beautiful
rirẹ (n) weakness
  i.e. in her weakness
ṣalanga (n) lavatory
  i.e. go to the lavatory

S

salubata (n) slippers
  i.e. you are wearing slippers

sanmọ (n) sky
  i.e. to fly into the sky
se (n) cast
  i.e. cast of a film
ṣe (v) make
  i.e. make food
ṣe giri (n) goosebumps
  i.e. I have got goosebumps

sekeseke (n) chain
  i.e. she has broken my chains
Ṣẹrẹ (n) January
  i.e. January has 31 days
sere (n) drop
  i.e. drop by drop a chicken drinks water
si (prep) to
  i.e. from here to there
ṣibi (n) spoon
  i.e. sixteen spoons
siga (n) cigarette
  i.e. smoke a cigarette
siga (n) cigarette
  i.e. smoke a cigarette
simbali (n) cymbal
  i.e. play the cymbals
simenti (n) cement
  i.e. stones and cement

singba (n) liberty
 i.e. we have liberty
sinima (n) cinema
 i.e. I am going to a cinema
sinima (n) cinema
 i.e. I am going to a cinema
sinki (n) sink
 i.e. drain the sink
sisọọsi (n) scissors
 i.e. give me the scissors
ṣokoleeti (n) chocolate
 i.e. the chocolate has become cheap
ṣọọsi (n) church
 i.e. go to church
sugbon (conj) but
 i.e. I like it, but

T

taba (n) tobacco
 i.e. smoke tobacco
taya (n) tyre
 i.e. roll a tyre
tẹlifonu (n) phone
 i.e. her phone

ti (prep) of
 i.e. language of Africa
tii (n) tea
 i.e. the tea is sweet
tikẹẹti (n) ticket
 i.e. look at my ticket
timtim (n) pillow
 i.e. pillow and bed
tirẹ (p) your
 i.e. your house
tomati (n) tomato
 i.e. two tomatoes
tutu (adj) cold
 i.e. cold water

U

ukulele (n) ukelele
 i.e. play the ukelele
un (n) thing
 i.e. the thing; the things

W

wa (v) come!
 i.e. come here!
wa (v) come
 i.e. to come here

wa (v) be
i.e. You are an important person
wahala (n) bother
i.e. too much bother
wakati (n) hour
i.e. ten hours
wẹ (v) bath
i.e. to bath each morning
wẹbusaiti (n) website
i.e. make a website for me
weefu (n) waves
i.e. the waves are breaking
wooli (n) prophet
i.e. powerful prophet
wọsẹ (n) sorcery
i.e. practise sorcery

ten me
yara ikeko (n) class
i.e. he is in class 2
yii (n) this
i.e. lend me this book
yọnda (v) allow
i.e. allow them
Yoruba (n) Yoruba
i.e. Yoruba language

Y

ya (v) borrow
i.e. borrow money
yan (v) bake
i.e. bake bread
yanmuyanmu (n) mosquito
i.e. a mosquito has bit-

Index

arrive *de*, 32
arrow *ọfa*, 44
as *bi*, 32
ash *eru*, 34
ask *bere*, 32
association *ẹgbẹ*, 33
at *ni*, 43
Ati Faranse ni mo ti wa,
    26
attach *fimọ*, 36
attire *aṣo*, 31
August *Ogun*, 45
award *ẹbun*, 33

baby *ọmọ-ọwọ*, 46
backyard *ẹyin-kule*, 35
bag *apo*, 30
bake *yan*, 51
ball *bọọlu*, 32
banana *ọgẹdẹ wẹrẹ*, 44
barrel *agba*, 28
basket *apẹrẹ*, 30
bath *wẹ*, 51
bathroom *ile iwẹ*, 39
battle *jagun*, 41
battle *ogun*, 45
Bawo ni?, 25
Bawo?, 25
be *wa*, 51

beach *eti okun*, 35
bean *ẹwa*, 35
beat *lu*, 43
beautiful *rẹwa*, 49
beauty *ẹwa*, 35
bed *ibusun*, 37
bedroom *iyara ibusun*, 41
beef *ẹran*, 34
behind *lẹhin*, 43
beloved *ayanfẹ*, 32
bicycle *kẹkẹ*, 42
bird *ẹiyẹ*, 33
bird *ẹyẹ*, 35
birthday *ọjọ ibi*, 45
bishop *olori awọn alufa*, 46
black *dudu*, 33
blanket *aṣọ ibora*, 31
bleeding *nṣẹjẹ*, 44
blessing *ibukun*, 37
blood *ẹjẹ*, 33
blow *fẹ*, 36
blow *iṣẹ*, 40
boat *ọkọ*, 45
book *iwe*, 41
borrow *ya*, 51
bother *wahala*, 51
bottle *igo*, 38
box *apoti*, 30
boy *ọmọkunrin*, 46

bread *burẹdi*, 32
breast *ọyọn*, 48
bride *iyawo*, 41
broom *igbalẹ*, 37
brother *arakunrin*, 31
brown *awo eeru*, 31
bucket *ike*, 38
build *ko*, 42
bum *idi*, 37
burglary *ole*, 46
burn *jo*, 42
bush *igbo*, 38
but *sugbon*, 50
butterfly *labalaba*, 42
buttocks *ikebe*, 38
Bẹẹko, 26
Bẹẹni, 26

canoe *oko oju omi*, 46
car *ọkọ ayọkẹlẹ*, 45
cassava *ege*, 33
cassava *paki*, 48
cast *se*, 49
cat *ologbo*, 46
cedi *ceedi*, 32
cement *simenti*, 49
certificate *iwe-eri*, 41
chain *sekeseke*, 49
chair *aga*, 28

character *iwa*, 41
charcoal *eedu*, 33
chest *aya*, 31
chew *je*, 42
chicken *adiyẹ*, 28
chieftain *oye*, 48
child *ọmọ*, 46
chin *agbon*, 29
chin *agbọn*, 29
chocolate *ṣokoleeti*, 50
christian *igbagbo*, 37
Christianity *onigbagbo*, 46
church *ile ijosin*, 39
church *ṣọọsi*, 50
cigarette *siga*, 49
cinema *sinima*, 50
citizen *omonilu*, 46
class *yara ikeko*, 51
clay *amọn*, 30
clean *fo*, 36
cloth *ewu*, 35
coach *kooṣi*, 42
cockerel *akukọ*, 29
cocoa *koko*, 42
cocoyam leaves *ewe koko*, 35
coin *fadaka*, 36
cold *tutu*, 50
collander *asẹ*, 31

comb *iyarun*, 41
come
   wa , 50
come *wa* , 50
comfort *alafia*, 30
compensation *itanran*, 40
competition *ere idije*, 34
computer *kọmpiyuta*, 42
concubine *ale*, 30
congratulations *oriire*, 47
Conjunctions, 16
consequence *abọ*, 28
consonants, 21
continent *orilẹ ede*, 47
coop *ago*, 29
corn *agbado*, 28
corners *origun*, 47
corpse *oku*, 46
court *kootu*, 42
covetuousness *aimojukuro*,
    29
cow *maalu*, 43
cowhide *pọnmọ*, 49
creation *ẹda*, 33
creator *ẹlẹda*, 34
crocodile *ọọni*, 47
crowd *ero*, 34
cup *ife*, 37
cutlass *ada*, 28

cymbal *simbali*, 49

Dakun, 26
day *ojumọ*, 45
daybreak *oju ojọ*, 45
December *Ọpẹ*, 47
deception *ẹtan*, 35
declarative sentences, 14
deer *ẹtu*, 35
determination *ifọkansi*, 37
diacritics, 18
digraphs, 22
discord *inunibini*, 39
disease *arun*, 31
disgrace *itiju*, 40
disposition *ero ọkan*, 34
diss *muṣere*, 43
division *pinpin*, 49
dog *aja*, 29
doll *ere*, 34
door *ilẹkun*, 39
dress *aṣọ*, 31
drop *sere*, 49
drum *ilu*, 39
duration *asiko*, 31
dustpan *ikolẹ*, 38

earth *orilẹ aye*, 47
eat *jẹ*, 42

Ebi npa mi, 26
education ẹkọ, 33
egg ẹyin, 35
elder agba, 28
elephant erin, 34
embrace dimọ, 32
empathy aanu, 28
encouragement iyanju, 41
end opin, 47
enemy ọta, 48
enmity inunibini, 39
evening irọlẹ, 39
event ayẹyẹ, 32
evil aida, 29
exam idanwo, 37
exultation ifiyin fun, 37
eye oju, 45
eyebrow irun oju, 40

face oju, 45
faith igbagbọ, 37
falsification ẹẹdan, 33
family ẹbi, 33
farm oko, 45
farmer agbẹ, 29
father baba, 32
fear ẹru, 34
feather iyẹ, 41
February Erele, 34

fees owo, 48
fence akọgba, 29
finger ika, 38
fish ẹja, 33
fisherman apẹja, 30
flesh ara ẹran, 30
floor ilẹ, 38
flour elubọ, 34
flower ododo, 44
fly fo, 36
food onje, 47
fool ọdẹ, 44
forehead iwaju ori, 41
foreigner ajeji, 29
forgetfulness igbagbe, 37
forgiveness idariji, 37
foundation ipilẹ, 39
friction ikọlu ara ẹni, 38
Friday Ẹti, 35
friend ọrẹ, 47
frog ọpọlọ, 47
from lati, 43
fruit eso, 35
funeral isinku, 40

game ere idaraya, 34
garden egg igba, 37
garment aṣọ, 31
generosity lawọ, 43

56

ghost *oku*, 46
gift *ẹbun*, 33
giraffe *agunfọn*, 29
girl *ọmọbinrin*, 46
glory *igbega*, 37
go *lọ*, 43
god *orisa*, 47
gong gong *gan gan*, 36
Good afternoon, 25
Good evening, 25
Good morning, 25
Good night, 25
Goodbye, 25
goosebumps *sẹ giri*, 49
gossip *gbeborun*, 36
government *ijọba*, 38
grammar, 7
gramme *iwọn giramu*, 41
grass *koriko*, 42
grease *ọmikin*, 46
groin *halahala*, 36
groundnut *ẹpa*, 34
group *ẹgbẹ*, 33
guest *alejo*, 30
gutter *gọta*, 36

habitual tense, 11
habit *iwa*, 40
habitat *ibugbe*, 36

hair *irun*, 40
hand *ọwọ*, 48
happiness *idunnu*, 37
hat *fila*, 36
hatred *ilara*, 38
head *ori*, 47
headgear *gele*, 36
health *ilera*, 39
heart *ọkan*, 45
Hello, 25
help *iranwọ*, 39
here *ibi*, 36
hiccups *esuke*, 35
hill *oke*, 45
history *adayeba*, 28
hoe *ọkọ*, 45
hole *iho*, 38
home *ile* , 38
hope *iforiti*, 37
horse *ẹsin*, 35
hotel *ile itura*, 39
hour *wakati*, 51
house *ile*, 38
How are you?, 25
human *eniyan*, 34
humankind *alara ẹran*, 30
hunger *ebi*, 33
husband *ọkọ*, 45
hydrogen *aidirogini*, 29

you *o*, 44
you *ę*, 33
your *tirę*, 50

http://kasahorow.org/yoruba

0-7 years

> My First Yoruba Dictionary

8-12 years

> 102 Yoruba Verbs
> Yoruba Children's Dictionary
> I Can Read Yoruba

12 years and over

> Modern Yoruba
> Yoruba Learner's Dictionary

Contact us: yoruba@kasahorow.org

Printed in Great Britain
by Amazon

75688974R00047